Contents

Note about the story

Doctor Who is a British TV series which was first **broadcast*** in 1963. The Doctor is an alien, but he looks like an ordinary man. He is the last of the Time Lords after they all disappeared in the Time Wars. He can live forever and travel in time and space. He works with a human **assistant** because he loves Earth and is very interested in humans.

The Doctor travels in a **TARDIS** (**T**ime **a**nd **R**elative **D**imension **i**n **S**pace). It can travel anywhere in time and space. The Doctor also uses a sonic screwdriver. It can lock and unlock doors and break and fix machines. Another useful thing is the Doctor's psychic paper – this is a piece of paper with nothing on it. When the Doctor shows it to someone, they see what he wants them to see on the piece of paper.

This story happens in London's Square Mile. This is in the centre of London and is called the City. The City holds all the big international banks and places where **traders** buy and sell things in a building called the stock market. People who work in the City often work long hours and make a lot of money, but they have little free time. Sometimes, people who work in banks and stock markets are called "**sharks**" because they seem not to care about people and they will do anything to make more money. The Time Market in this story is like a stock market in the real world, but traders buy and sell time instead of money.

Before-reading questions

1 Look at the cover of the book. What do you think the story will be about?

2 Look at the pictures in the book. Describe the characters. Who are they, do you think, and what will happen to them?

3 Look up the words "stock market" in your dictionary. What do you know about how stock markets work?

4 How much time do people in your country spend at work? How much time is too long to spend working, do you think?

5 The story is about time travel. Time travel causes something called a "paradox". Find out what "paradox" means.

6 Read the back cover of the book. What do you think will happen in the story? Choose the correct sentences.
  a Andrew Brown will borrow time from some aliens.
  b Borrowing time will make Andrew Brown's life easier.
  c The Doctor won't help Andrew Brown.
  d Some people in the story will travel in time.

*Definitions of words in **bold** can be found in the glossary on pages 92–96.

CHAPTER ONE
All the time you want

Mr Symington and Mr Blenkinsop entered Andrew Brown's life on possibly his worst morning at Lexington International Bank. He had spent ten years trying to climb the **career ladder**. Most days, he sat in front of a computer for twelve hours and made guesses about other people's money. Did he really want to get to the top of the ladder? Well, everyone at the bank was climbing it, so he hoped that he would like the top when he arrived there.

And now there was a chance of a **promotion**, which would mean more important meetings, with more important people. Then, one day, he might get another promotion, and then . . . one day he would be the **boss** of the whole office. Andrew could not remember why he wanted to be the boss, but, anyway, it was important to have a dream.

Today's meeting was very important. The new boss of the London office, Vanessa Laing-Randall, would be there. If he **impressed** her, then that promotion was one step closer. But he had competition for the promotion: the always well-**prepared** Sameera Jenkins. She always knew more than Andrew and had always worked just one extra hour on a **presentation**. But, this time, no one could be better prepared than Andrew Brown.

He woke up on the morning of the meeting feeling well rested and calm . . . "Wait a minute," he thought.

"Why am I well rested? Why am I calm?" He was suddenly very afraid. He had slept for too long! It was 6:45 a.m. He jumped out of bed, ran to the bathroom and washed his face quickly. Then he picked up his suit from the chair and knocked a glass of water over the trousers.

"Oh no!" he shouted at no one. Then he put the suit on anyway, and he ran for the train. From the station, he ran all the way to the office. When he saw that the lifts were full, he ran up the stairs to the seventh floor. He arrived, hot and breathing hard, with just enough time to see perfect Sameera Jenkins finish her presentation. He was too late; the meeting was finished. He heard clapping from his boss, and his boss's boss and Vanessa Laing-Randall herself.

Andrew Brown tried not to cry. He had lost his chance to impress Vanessa. He walked back to his office, where he sat and laid his head on his desk.

And then, suddenly, two white men, dressed in the same black suits and white shirts, were in his office. They had the kind of boring faces that you would forget the moment they left the room.

"Good morning," said one. "I'm Mr Symington. This is Mr Blenkinsop."

"Good morning to you, Mr Andrew Brown," said the other man. "Although, in fact, we hear you've had a bad morning."

"Everyone has a bad morning sometimes," said Mr Symington. "Luckily for you, we're here to help."

"Help?" Andrew asked.

"We have something very special for you, Mr Brown," said Mr Blenkinsop. "Something that will help you with your bad morning and every bad morning you will ever have in the future."

Mr Symington continued, "How would you feel if you could get an extra hour any time you liked? An extra hour for that report for your boss, or to spend time with your loved ones or just to sleep late?"

"Just think of it," said Mr Blenkinsop. "Everyone knows that an hour before breakfast **is worth** three hours in the afternoon. Think about today, for example. Wouldn't you happily give me the rest of the day if I could give you two extra hours this morning? There would be no stopping you from climbing up the career ladder then, would there, Mr Brown?"

Mr Symington spoke again. "Mr Brown, we can lend you enough time to prepare for this morning's meeting. The time to spend with friends and family. The time to get ahead of Sameera Jenkins. But, of course, Mr Brown, that time will have to be paid back."

"At a very fair **interest rate**," said Mr Blenkinsop, so fast that Andrew did not hear him.

And, suddenly, Andrew Brown felt very angry. Here he was, on the worst day of his life, and these men were making stupid jokes. "Lend me . . . what on earth are you talking about? Look, how did you get in here? Who are you?" he shouted.

"He doesn't believe us," said Mr Blenkinsop.

"They never do," replied Mr Symington.

"I think we should show him, Mr Symington," said Mr Blenkinsop. He took something from his pocket. And then Andrew Brown understood everything.

Fifty-first-century Earth was definitely a beautiful place to spend a holiday, Amy thought. She was inside a large Special Time **Bubble** on a beach covered with white sand, and she was watching the sun go down. For three hours, the sky had been filled with gold and orange. Out at sea, a big fish jumped in the air, happy to be alive. Amy silently thanked the Doctor for agreeing to her three-week holiday from work and walked over to the edge of the Bubble. The Bubble shook, and the orange sky seemed to shake, too.

She looked down at her new, pink Special Lucky Holiday Camera: Catch the Moment!™ It had a **cosmic radiation battery** that took **energy** from the **universe**, so the battery never needed **recharging**. Every time she used the camera, it made a Time Bubble around her. Time inside the Time Bubble went faster, while things outside the Time Bubble seemed slower. Thanks to the Time Bubble, she already felt like she had been on holiday for weeks.

But then she heard a loud noise.

Vworp, vworp, vworp.

The **TARDIS** suddenly appeared inside the Time Bubble, and the door opened. "Did you have a good three weeks?" asked the Doctor.

"It hasn't been three weeks!" said Amy.

The Doctor pulled an enormous watch from his pocket. He looked at it. "Not three weeks?" he said. "Time goes quickly when you're having fun, but, yes, it's three weeks . . . now! Time to get back to work!"

"Doctor!" shouted Amy. "It's only been six days! Look, I'm using this camera to make Time Bubbles."

She gave him the camera, and he looked at it quickly.

"Well, it's only been six days in Earth time, but inside the Time Bubble it's been three weeks." The Doctor pushed a button, and the Time Bubble disappeared. Then he threw the camera back to Amy. "Keep that. It could be useful. Right! Come with me!"

Amy followed the Doctor into the TARDIS with the camera in her hand.

"We are going to Lexington International Bank," he continued, "to save the future of this beautiful Earth!" He pointed outside the doors. Then he turned around in a circle, pushed two buttons and the TARDIS disappeared again.

CHAPTER TWO
Strange things happen at Lexington International Bank

London's Square Mile was the home of Lexington International Bank. People in expensive suits walked through the **atrium** and past a large, glass **sculpture** with the words "Time is money" written at the bottom. In the **basement**, there was a noise – *vworp, vworp, vworp* – and a blue box with a light on top of it appeared.

––––––––

The Doctor opened the TARDIS door and got out. "Come on!" he called to Amy, who was wearing clothes for work in a bank. "We've got places to go to, people to meet and the Earth to save!"

He put his head out of the door of the room, looked left and right, and walked out. Then he led Amy towards a door that opened on to the street outside.

"But," said Amy, "aren't we already inside the bank?"

"This is a bank!" said the Doctor. "The receptionist has to let us in!" And they walked round to the front of the bank.

"Please," said a voice by their feet. "Please . . ."

Sitting outside the front doors of the bank was an old woman. She was wearing a dirty coat, although her shoes looked expensive. She looked very tired, like she had not slept for days. Strangely, she was wearing a **name badge** that said "Nadia Montgomery, **Head of Communications**".

She pulled at the Doctor's coat. "Can you help me?"

Amy pulled some money out of the pocket of her suit and gave it to the woman. "Here," she said, "have this."

The woman looked at the money like she did not understand what it was. "Time is money," she said. "Money is time; you can give me one but you can't give the other."

Amy didn't understand what the woman was talking about.

"That was kind, Amy," said the Doctor. "But we've got a bank to **inspect**."

"Don't go in there!" the woman shouted. "They'll steal your time, and you'll never get it back."

The Doctor turned back round. "What did you say about time?" he asked her.

The old woman stared at the Doctor. "I can't remember," she said. "I feel so old." And then she stopped talking and stared at nothing instead. There was nothing more Amy and the Doctor could do to help Nadia, if that really was her name, so they walked into the bank.

"I'm the Doctor," said the Doctor, smiling at the receptionist. "And this is Amy Pond." He waved his psychic paper in front of the receptionist's face. The psychic paper made the receptionist see what the Doctor wanted her to see. "As you can see, we're here to inspect the bank. We want to know if your workers are happy."

The receptionist checked the paper and smiled at them. "Good morning, Doctor Schmidt," she said. "I'll just let Ms Laing-Randall know that you are here."

"As you can see, Doctor Schmidt," said Vanessa Laing-Randall as she finished showing them the offices of Lexington Bank and returned to the atrium, "we are a good bank, and our workers are very happy. Do you know the **Chancellor of the Exchequer** will be giving a speech from our office tomorrow? Do you see that sculpture?"

The sculpture looked like several trees **twisted** around each other, with their branches twisting up to the top of the atrium. There was a strange light at the centre of the sculpture, making it look alive.

"That's not just a sculpture," said Vanessa. "It shows how we, here at Lexington, see the different parts of life at the bank. We believe that each part is equally important. People must plan their work and their life outside work . . ."

While Vanessa continued talking about life at the bank, Amy looked through the atrium's glass walls. She could see busy people everywhere, except for one man opposite her, across the atrium. He was standing in front of his computer with his head in his hands. Then he turned, and Amy saw that he looked angry and afraid. Then he looked down at his **wrist** and touched something on it. Suddenly, he fell to the floor.

Amy and the Doctor ran around to his office as quickly as they could.

But, by the time they got there, a secretary had already covered his face with a coat. She was standing, shocked, by the dead body.

"Doctor," whispered Amy, "I saw him do something just before he died. He touched something on his wrist – I think it was a watch."

"He worked too much," said Vanessa Laing-Randall, who had followed them. She was looking down at the man. "We encourage people to take holidays, but sometimes they don't do it. A quarter of our staff didn't use all their holidays last year. Mr –" she looked at her phone – "Brian Edelman here hasn't taken a day's holiday in eighteen months."

The Doctor looked down at the body. "Hmm. Did you say he was looking at his watch?" He gently pulled away the coat to check the man's wrists. There was no watch on either wrist.

"Well, I thought I saw –" Amy began.

"You were on the other side of the atrium, Ms Pond," said Vanessa.

"Then," said the Doctor, "I think my **assistant** and I will have to inspect the bank a little longer."

Vanessa tried to look pleased. "Yes, of course."

She moved him away from the body. "It's a terrible shock. Nothing like this has happened before, Doctor Schmidt."

"It's lucky that we're here today, Ms Laing-Randall," said the Doctor. "We can check that no one is working as hard as **poor** Brian Edelman. Amy, go and talk to some other **managers**. We need to know if they are working too hard." He moved closer to Amy and whispered in her ear, "And what kind of watches they wear."

He stood up straight and spoke more loudly. "I will come with you, Vanessa Laing-Randall, because I think that you might be doing something quite interesting and . . . dangerous."

"I've got a meeting with **clients** from PZP Group," Vanessa replied, "if that's what you mean? I don't think anyone would call it dangerous."

"I don't mean PZP Group are dangerous," said the Doctor. "But, anyway, let's go to the meeting! We haven't got any time to lose, have we?"

Amy walked around the building, looking for people drinking tea. Where there was tea, there was always office **gossip**. She soon heard how Vanessa had appeared suddenly about six months ago, from the Hong Kong office. Since then, there had been a lot more work to do in the London office. Someone said that one of the top managers had been in two cities at the same time – a meeting in Tokyo in the morning, then New York in the afternoon. Amy only knew one man who could be in Tokyo one minute and New York the next. That was the Doctor. She thought maybe she was starting to understand what was happening at Lexington Bank.

But the strangest thing she heard was when she was crossing the hall between two offices. On one side of the hall was a man in a blue shirt talking on the phone.

"I'm waiting for some very important documents from Stockholm," he was saying. "Aren't they here yet?"

And that was strange because, across the hall, someone who looked just like him was shouting at a secretary. Amy could hear only a few of his words: "... copy ... now ... **tax** laws ... Delaware ..."

Something strange was definitely happening.

CHAPTER THREE
The watches that lend time

"Doctor, what are you doing?" asked Vanessa. She had brought the Doctor to her important client meeting, just like he had asked.

The Doctor did not answer and continued to search the meeting room. The people who were sitting around the huge table in the middle of the room were **confused**. They watched the Doctor search along the walls and the windows, and then around the drinks cupboard.

"Doctor," Vanessa said, "we have to start this meeting now. Please could you sit down and do that later, while we win some business that will bring £300 million to the bank?"

"Oh, yes, of course," he said, and he sat down just as the American clients arrived. The first presentation started well. Andrew Brown had spent a lot of time preparing his presentation, and it was very good. But then one of the American women said, "When Morgan Stanley gave us their presentation, they talked about the tax laws."

"The tax . . . ?" Andrew asked, and he smiled in a very strange way.

"The tax laws in Delaware," she repeated. "They're extremely important."

Andrew Brown made his smile nicer. "Oh, yes," he said, "I've actually prepared a document about that. Just give me a moment, and I'll be right back with it."

It really was only a moment; the clients were very impressed. In less time than it would take to walk down the hall, he came back carrying the documents. He gave them to the Americans, who looked at them and smiled.

The Doctor looked at Vanessa. "Your team is very fast," he said.

Then Sameera gave her presentation. When the clients asked a difficult IT question, she left the room for a few seconds and returned to give an excellent **demonstration**. Everyone clapped when she finished, and Andrew Brown looked at her like he hated her.

"That was great," said one of the American men, smiling. "Amazing. The best birthday gift ever."

"It's your birthday?" Sameera asked. "But of course . . . we've got a cake for you. Just wait here."

The clients thought she was joking. She was not. The Doctor guessed that she left the room for 12.8 seconds, and then she returned with a huge cake with the words "Happy Birthday, Greg!" on the top.

"That's impossible!" said the Doctor to Vanessa.

"It's all because, thanks to me, my managers are all excellent at managing their time," said Vanessa.

"I'm sure it is," said the Doctor. He stared hard at her face. "And I'm going to learn what 'managing time' means in Lexington International Bank!"

"Would you like some birthday cake, Doctor?" asked Vanessa.

The Doctor suddenly smiled warmly. "Yes, please. I never say no to birthday cake."

He took a piece and, with his mouth full, said, "This cake is amazing – I don't know where Sameera got it from, or should I say 'when'? I have to tell Amy. May I?" The Doctor pulled the phone from Vanessa's hand. "Ah, **voicemail** . . . Pond!" he said. "You have to get up here right now . . . it's important. Come up to the tenth floor right now!"

When her phone rang, Amy did not answer it. She was in Sameera Jenkins's office, looking through Sameera's desk for **evidence**. If the managers were suddenly working extra hard, perhaps harder than was actually possible, the evidence for how they were achieving it all must be in one of these offices. Sameera's desk was filled with papers and receipts. They were not very interesting . . . except . . . how strange. The receipts showed that Sameera had bought lunch five times in two hours yesterday, all at the same shop. Then Amy found a notebook with lists of dates and clothes. Amy looked at today: *Tuesday, dark blue suit, pink blouse, tiny green mark on left pocket.*

"What do you think you're doing?" said a voice. Sameera was back from her meeting.

Amy stood up suddenly and hit her head on the desk. "I . . ." she said. "Look, it's not what it looks like . . ." Amy noticed that Sameera was wearing a dark blue suit and a pink blouse with a tiny green mark on the left pocket.

Sameera reached for the phone. "I'm going to call

22

someone, and they'll make you leave," she said.

Amy saw something on Sameera's wrist. It was a watch – or something like a watch – with several **dials** moving at different speeds. Amy knew that she was looking at **alien technology**. She tried to hold Sameera's wrist so she could get a better look at the watch.

"What's this, Sameera?" she said. "I'm sure it's something you don't want your bosses to know about . . ."

"No!" shouted Sameera and pulled her hand away.

"You're a **time traveller**!" said Amy.

"It's just for work," Sameera said. "How did you know?"

"I'm a time traveller, too," said Amy.

Sameera did not say anything more about calling anyone. She seemed happy to have someone to talk to.

"Don't you think," asked Sameera, "that eating lunch is a real problem? I forget how many hours I've spent awake and what I've already eaten. I spend so much money on sandwiches."

"I think I time-travel in a different way from you. How does your watch work?" asked Amy.

"It's really easy," Sameera said. "You just turn this dial here to get more time. I suppose I should do it less often, but there's so much to do. Andrew Brown is trying to get the same promotion as me, and I want that job! For a while, I was winning, but these last few weeks he's got ahead of me. I think he's got a watch, too. Who do you borrow your time from?"

"Borrow?" said Amy. Then her phone started ringing.

"Pond!" said the Doctor's voice. "You have to come here right now!"

"Doctor, I can't, I –" Amy said.

"Oh, it doesn't matter! It's too late!" He ended the call.

"I've missed something important," Amy said in a worried voice.

"It sounds," said Sameera, "like you need to borrow some time."

CHAPTER FOUR
Amy tries a watch

Amy knew that going back again and again to change the same moment in history was dangerous. "But," she thought, "it's probably only changing big, important moments that is dangerous, not little things at work. So maybe the watch is quite safe to use."

"Totally safe," said Mr Symington.

"We're sure of it," said Mr Blenkinsop. "We would hate to lose a customer, wouldn't we?"

Then Mr Symington and Mr Blenkinsop both laughed. They had arrived, surprisingly quickly, because Sameera had called them with her watch. And they were very happy to give Amy a watch and lend her some time, too.

Mr Symington put it on her wrist and showed her how to use it. "Move this dial back to borrow time," he said. "And **press** this button to pay it back."

"Pay it back?" Amy asked.

"Well, of course." Mr Blenkinsop smiled, warmly. "We can't give our time away, can we? We think you'll agree our interest rate is very fair – just five minutes per hour."

"Per hour," agreed Mr Symington.

"The time comes off your life, but," Mr Blenkinsop laughed, "are you really going to miss an extra five minutes?"

"It's the sort of time you might spend watching adverts on TV," said Mr Symington. "Or staring at nothing."

Amy knew that she should ask the Doctor. But, if she called him, he would be angry with her because she had not gone to him when he had called her earlier.

A long message suddenly appeared on the watch's glass face. It was written in very small letters, with big letters at the end saying: **IF YOU ACCEPT THE TERMS AND CONDITIONS, press OK.**

"So just press here, and you're ready," said Mr Blenkinsop.

"Just do it," said Sameera. "No one reads **terms and conditions**, do they?"

Amy's phone started to ring again. It was the Doctor. "Oh, all right then!" she said, and she pressed "OK".

———————

Amy had to admit that it was exciting to put the watch back an hour.

She was still in Sameera's office with Mr Symington and Mr Blenkinsop, but Sameera had not arrived back yet.

"Miss Jenkins isn't here yet," said Mr Blenkinsop. "It's 1 p.m., Ms Pond – lunch hour is just beginning, and you can do anything you want with your extra time."

"The Doctor is going to be very pleased," Amy thought, and she bought herself a nice lunch in a restaurant near the bank. She was quite pleased with herself, too. She had almost found the answers to the **mystery**, hadn't she? "This is why Andrew Brown was in two places at the same time," she thought. "It's because he was using the watch. And Brian Edelman did the same thing. Maybe it's like Vanessa said: there is too much work."

"I'll go and talk to the Doctor now," she thought after her lunch. "I'll learn what he wanted that was so important. Then I can show him the watch, which will explain everything, and then we can leave this stupid bank." She stood in the atrium and turned her watch back two more hours.

It felt nice. It was like getting two extra hours of sleep but all in one second so you really felt recharged. Without really thinking, she turned it back another hour. Suddenly, it was only 11 a.m.

She looked at herself in the glass of the atrium's windows. Her hair was very long. It needed a cut.

And so she spent the rest of the morning, or the day, or . . . it was very confusing. So far, she had taken four hours, so she **owed** about twenty minutes of her life. That was fine. "I wouldn't like to owe more than a week," she decided. So, how many five minutes in a week? "There are twelve in an hour. So, 12 x 24 hours in a day x 7 days in a week = 2,016," she thought. "That's how many five-minute pieces of time I would be happy to pay." And so that was how many hours she would be happy to borrow: 2,016 hours. Eighty-four days. Nearly three months. That was . . . an exciting amount of time!

She decided three months was probably more than she needed, but there were still so many things she could do. She turned the dial on the watch back twenty-four hours this time. That felt amazing. It was like a whole day of sleep. She rented a car and drove to her parents' house.

Her parents were happy to see her, and she fell asleep in

the same bed she had slept in when she was a child. When she woke up at 8 a.m., her mum was doing the washing-up. Downstairs, she could hear her dad mending the cooker. "Maybe I'll stay a bit longer . . ." Amy thought, and she turned the watch back another two hours. The nice feeling filled her body again. She went downstairs, and, by the time her mum got up, Amy had done the washing-up, made breakfast and picked some flowers from the garden for the living-room table. She had even mended the cooker.

———

Back in London, she planned to go immediately to meet the Doctor. What had he called her about? He had not said, but it sounded important. Then, suddenly, she realized she had left yesterday's work clothes at her parents' house, and she was wearing a skirt, boots and a bright red sweater. Now she understood why Sameera wrote what she was wearing every day in her notebook. She could not go into a bank in these clothes, so she turned the watch back again. She needed time to go shopping.

Before she knew it, she was really tired even though it was only 10 a.m. She had turned back so much time that she had been awake for almost twenty-four hours. Well, she could not meet the Doctor while she was so tired. She turned the dial back one more time, and now it was last night again.

She walked to the nearest hotel and booked a room for the night.

When she woke up in the hotel's big, soft bed, she could not stop thinking of all the things she could do with the watch. She could make time to get a present for the Doctor. Or maybe she could go to Lexington Bank a few days earlier and leave something for him to find. That would be so funny! Or maybe . . . Then she stopped herself and stared at the watch. This was all a bit too easy, wasn't it? Where had all that time gone? She **wondered** how much time she had borrowed. She added it all together – well, as much as she could remember, anyway. Her hair, visiting her parents, shopping, last night . . . The total was about four days, she thought. Five minutes of interest per hour was a total of 480 minutes of interest. She owed 104 hours. It was enough. She was still late to meet the Doctor. When she arrived at the bank, it was 1:20 p.m., and she had already missed his call to her mobile phone. She thought about turning the watch back so that she could arrive in time for 1 p.m. But she felt a bit sick when she thought of where the last four days had gone.

"Pond!" shouted the Doctor from the meeting room as she walked out of the lift on to the tenth floor. "You're late. And you haven't tried any of this lovely cake yet, and you haven't . . ." He stopped talking and stared at her. The Doctor put his face very close to hers, then looked around her and behind her. Then he held her wrist so that he could see the watch.

"Oh, Pond," he said. "What have you done?"

CHAPTER FIVE
Chocolate cake and interest rates

"This watch is a Time **Harvester**," said the Doctor. "If you use it, it will take time from you, and you really don't want that to happen." He was walking up and down, shaking his head.

"But, Doctor, it doesn't work like that," Amy said. "It lets me borrow time. I've only borrowed about four days. The interest is only about eight hours! It's nothing!"

"Oh, Amy," the Doctor said, very quietly. He pulled at her wrist again and pressed a button on the watch. A message came up that said:

BORROWED TIME TOTAL: 4 DAYS, 3 HOURS.

"That's what I said," said Amy. "Four days. I pay five minutes of interest for each hour, so I only need to pay back eight hours of interest. It's fine! I'll pay it back now if you just let me press the button." Then she reached for the button that Mr Symington and Mr Blenkinsop had shown her.

"No, don't!" shouted the Doctor. "Look at the interest!"

The message had changed.

INTEREST TERMS: FIVE MINUTES PER HOUR, PER HOUR

"That's what I said," said Amy.

"No, you said five minutes per hour," he said. "That's a very different thing. Let me explain."

He picked up a pen and started to draw on the glass wall of the atrium. "Five minutes per hour, right? Imagine you've borrowed a hundred hours." He wrote: *5 x 100 = 500.*

"That means you would owe 500 minutes' interest. The problem is that it's not five minutes per hour, it's five minutes per hour, every hour."

Amy started to have a bad feeling. "So that's . . . five minutes per hour, every hour," Amy said, slowly. She took the pen and wrote: *5 x 100 x 100 =.* "That makes . . . 50,000? I owe 50,000 minutes?!" she shouted.

"Amy, it's much worse than that," he said. "You pay interest on the interest, also called **compound interest**. Compound interest is why people can't pay back their credit cards. This is how poor people stay poor and rich people get rich. It's . . . look at this cake." He pointed at the enormous cake on the table.

The Doctor cut a piece of cake with thick chocolate **icing** on the top. "The cake, this yellow part, is the hour of time you've borrowed. And the icing is the interest. So this piece is one hour. Now let's borrow another hour." He cut another piece of cake. "One more piece of cake. Plus the icing as interest. Plus you owe an extra piece of icing because you've got two pieces of cake, right? Every hour, you have to pay one piece of icing for every piece of cake you've borrowed. Two hours, two pieces of icing."

He made a gentle cut on top of the cake and cut off an extra piece of icing, leaving the cake partly **bare**. He put the icing on top of the second piece of cake. "That's what you owe. Now let's borrow another hour." He cut another piece of cake with icing. "Now the interest." He cut two more pieces of icing and put them on top of the second piece of cake.

"There's almost more icing than cake now!" said Amy.

"That," the Doctor said, "is what I am trying to show you. Let's borrow another hour." He cut another piece, and then he cut three more pieces of icing.

He put all the extra icing together with the icing he had already cut.

Now there was a whole extra piece of cake just made of icing.

"So now, if you borrow another piece of cake, how many pieces of icing will we have to take?" the Doctor said, and he cut another piece of cake.

Amy counted the pieces. "There are five pieces of cake, so we need five pieces of icing," she said.

"Plus the piece made completely out of icing," he said. "That's six. So we have to cut an extra piece of icing. But six pieces of icing is the same as a whole extra piece. That means that every time you borrow another piece, you get a whole extra piece just made of icing."

Amy felt sick. The cake was almost completely bare.

"Once an hour, you get a piece of icing for every hour that you've borrowed. That's how compound interest works. The icing you have to pay on the icing becomes thousands of times more than the cake. I'm sorry, Amy, but you owe ten years."

"You must have made a mistake," Amy said. "I only borrowed four days."

He shook his head, sadly. "Even if you don't borrow any more time, it's going up by about a year an hour now."

She was shaking. "Get it off me!" she screamed. She picked up the knife and tried to push the watch off.

She cut herself, but she did not care about the blood.

"Amy!" the Doctor shouted, and he tried to take the knife before she hurt herself more.

"Is there a problem?" said Mr Symington, from very close behind her.

She screamed again. Suddenly, from nowhere, the two men were in the meeting room.

"We hope you weren't trying to take off your watch," said Mr Blenkinsop. "You remember the terms and conditions? If you try to remove a Time-Harvester watch, you immediately owe us your whole lifetime."

Mr Symington's smile grew bigger, and his mouth opened much wider than any human mouth could open. The mouth was filled with teeth that looked like blood-red **shark's** teeth. His skin was turning grey like a shark's, too.

"Run!" the Doctor shouted.

They ran out of the meeting room, towards the lifts. Mr Symington and Mr Blenkinsop followed them. Amy threw some office chairs behind her as she ran, and Mr Symington fell, which gave Amy and the Doctor enough time to reach the lift.

"We have to get back to the TARDIS," said the Doctor.

"If we can get out of here, we can think about how to get that thing off your wrist when we're a thousand years away."

"Can't they take the time out of my watch anyway?" said Amy.

The Doctor pressed a button on the watch and read some of the terms and conditions.

"It says that they have to take your time **in person**," he said. "If you stay away from them, they can't take your time."

They reached the ground floor, and the lift doors opened. Mr Symington and Mr Blenkinsop were waiting in the atrium. For a moment the two shark-men did not notice Amy and the Doctor. When they did, their heads turned at the same moment. Amy and the Doctor ran out of the building, and she pulled the Doctor towards the restaurant where she had had lunch four days ago and was having lunch right now. She could see the other Amy, and, as they ran past, she felt her **memory** changing. Yes, she suddenly remembered that she had seen herself and the Doctor run past when she was having lunch, and she had wondered what was happening. Or had that new memory only just appeared?

They went behind the back of the building. "We can't lose them while you're wearing that watch. It's telling them where you are," the Doctor said. "If we can get to the TARDIS, maybe we can . . ."

Suddenly, Mr Symington and Mr Blenkinsop came

35

down the road. They saw the Doctor and Amy and started to run towards them.

"I've got an idea," said Amy, and she pulled the Special Lucky Holiday Camera out of her pocket. Usually, you turned the camera towards yourself. But she held it the other way round, pointing it at Mr Symington and Mr Blenkinsop. She pressed the camera's button, and a Time Bubble grew around the two shark-men.

"Good thinking, Amy," said the Doctor. They walked around the corner towards the basement where they had left the TARDIS. Waiting by the door were Mr Symington and Mr Blenkinsop. Across the road was another pair of Mr Symington and Mr Blenkinsop. Further up the street, towards the front door, there they were again. At the same moment, all three pairs of Mr Symington and Mr Blenkinsop turned their heads and saw the Doctor and Amy. Then they started to run towards the Doctor and Amy again, with their sharks' mouths open.

CHAPTER SIX
Run! Sharks!

Amy picked up a stone from the ground and threw it hard at the nearest shark-man. He cried out, and she saw a red cut on his cheek. Cuts suddenly appeared on the cheeks of all the other Mr Symingtons and Mr Blenkinsops.

Then there was a sudden noise and a bright light and the sound of a woman shouting. The shark-men all turned to see what was happening. The old woman from outside the office, Nadia, was standing with her left arm high in the air, waving it around. She was wearing a watch on her wrist, like Amy's, but **sparks** were coming out of it.

All the Mr Symingtons and Mr Blenkinsops started moving like an army towards the old woman.

"Over here!" Nadia shouted, waving her arm above her head. "Come on!"

"Now!" the Doctor said.

Amy pointed the camera at each pair of shark-men and pressed several times. The three pairs of shark-men were caught in three Time Bubbles.

"That was amazing!" said Amy to Nadia. Nadia had looked like a young woman when she was shouting at the sharks, but now she just looked old. Her wrist was red where the watch was hurting it. More sparks came from Nadia's watch and made the skin on her arm redder. She held out her arm towards Amy. "The watch is broken."

The Doctor pulled a small black machine out of his pocket and held it near Nadia's watch. He nodded. "You're right, Nadia. It is broken. And it must hurt. Look." He pointed to a little hole in the side of Nadia's watch where the sparks came from. "Something went wrong when they made this one. Can you see the dial?"

It was hard to look at the dial on Nadia's watch. For a moment the dial was there, and then it disappeared for a second or two. "That's why the Mr Symingtons and Mr Blenkinsops can't see you until you call them, isn't it? They look for the watch, but the watch is coming and going in time."

Nadia nodded. She looked even older now.

"And it's taking time from you and giving it back," the Doctor added. "So you keep getting older and younger."

Nadia nodded, sadly. "Can you make this stop and give me my time back?" she asked the Doctor.

One of the Time Bubbles with a Mr Symington and Mr Blenkinsop inside was starting to move more than the others. It only had a few minutes left before it disappeared.

"Yes, I can," the Doctor said. "Do you think you can help us, too?"

Nadia looked at the Doctor. She was a bit younger again. "Yes," she replied.

"Then let's go," said the Doctor.

When they got near the bank, the Doctor said, "Nadia, I need you to go into the basement and watch the TARDIS for me. I don't think that the aliens can get inside the TARDIS, but I need to know if they try to break it."

Nadia hated going into the bank. She was afraid of it now that she was old and confused. She went as quickly as she could and tried not to let anyone see her. In the basement, there were hundreds of Mr Symingtons and Mr Blenkinsops, but they could not see her. They were all staring at the big blue TARDIS in the corner.

Some of them were touching and pulling its doors, but they could not open them. Nadia sat quietly in the dark at the back of the room and sent a message to Amy's phone to tell her what had happened.

"We can't go into the basement," said the Doctor as he and Amy walked away from the bank. "It's too dangerous for us if they know what the TARDIS is. It's even worse if they can time travel."

Amy did not understand. "Why can't we just run into the basement, open the TARDIS and get away?" she asked.

"Because," he said, "if we try to get to the TARDIS, they will travel back in time for a few minutes and will be waiting for us. But, it's not all bad news. We've learned something about our shark friends. All the Mr Symingtons and Mr Blenkinsops suddenly got a cut on their cheeks when you hit one of them with the stone, right? That's because they're all the same person! Do you remember how they all turned their heads to look at us at the same time? When one of them sees us, then all the others that come later know where we are, because they remember it in their own past."

Suddenly, three Mr Symingtons and a Mr Blenkinsop

40

came round the corner.

Amy and the Doctor immediately ran into a park and hid behind some trees. The Doctor held Amy's wrist and pointed the sonic screwdriver at it.

"What are you doing, Doctor?" asked Amy.

"Breaking your new watch," he said.

He pressed three buttons on Amy's watch and pointed his sonic screwdriver at it again. Sparks came from the watch and flew into the air towards the bank. The Mr Symingtons and Mr Blenkinsop stopped and looked round at the sparks. Then they all turned and ran towards the bank.

"Are we safe now, Doctor?" asked Amy.

The Doctor opened his eyes very wide. "No," he said, "Earth is not going to be safe until the very last one – or actually I mean the very FIRST one – of those aliens is gone. But if you mean, 'Are they going to try to kill us in the next twenty minutes?' then, yes, we're safe."

"So," said Amy, staring at her watch, "why did you do it?"

"I broke your watch to make it act the same as Nadia's broken watch. A bit of your time is now back at the bank, so that is where the Mr Symingtons and Mr Blenkinsops think that you are. Now do you understand?"

"No," said Amy.

"We're safe for now," said the Doctor, speaking very slowly, "but we have to learn which of the Mr Symingtons and Mr Blenkinsops came first. Then we need to travel back in time and stop them from giving the Time-Harvester watches to everyone.

"Plus, we need to find where they're **storing** the time that they have taken from people. It's very difficult to store time. We need to find the **storage** and **deactivate** it. Do you understand that?"

"Do you mean," asked Amy, "that we have to stop the shark-men and get everyone's time back?"

"Yes, that's what I mean, Amy!" said the Doctor. "But, first, we need a friend who works in the bank. They need to look for evidence and documents that explain what's happening and who first brought those watches to the bank. The best person would be someone who is part of this already. Maybe someone who has borrowed more time than they realize."

"Andrew Brown!" said Amy. "I've seen him in two different places at the same time in the bank. He's probably borrowed too much time."

CHAPTER SEVEN

Where do aliens store things?

"Give me your phone, Amy," the Doctor said. He took the phone, pressed it a few times and then said, "Aha! Google really is as good as some of the alien technology. Here's Andrew Brown's address."

Half an hour later, they were walking down a street in North London, looking for Andrew Brown's house.

"How do we know that he'll be here, Doctor?" said Amy. "It's a work day."

Her question was answered when they saw Andrew's flat. He was everywhere on it and in it. There was an Andrew Brown on a ladder painting the windows. A different Andrew Brown was taking out the rubbish, and another Andrew Brown was cleaning the car.

Inside the house, they could see an Andrew Brown cooking in the kitchen. One was walking up the path to the front door as another was walking out of the house.

"Excuse me?" said the Doctor to the group of Andrew Browns.

Several of the Andrew Browns turned round at the same time. The Andrew Brown who was washing the car smiled. "I know you from the bank, don't I?" he said. "Doctor Schmidt from Zurich? How can I help you?" The other Andrew Browns went back to what they were doing.

"That's clever," said the Doctor to Amy. "He's the

earliest. The others remember that he talked to me, so they don't have to listen to know what we say."

The Doctor caught Andrew's wrist and held Andrew's watch up to his ear. "How much time have you borrowed, Andrew?" the Doctor asked him.

Andrew stared at the Doctor and then looked at Amy, who smiled. He took a deep breath.

"A few days, I think. Not more than a week. And I paid a little bit back once, but . . ."

"Yes, it doesn't feel nice when you pay it back, but it feels nice to borrow it. I totally understand," said the Doctor. "I think you've borrowed more time than that, Andrew."

"Well, maybe ten days?" Andrew guessed. "Or a couple of weeks?"

The Doctor pressed a button on the watch, and a message appeared:

BORROWED TIME TOTAL: 9 DAYS, 1 HOUR.
INTEREST TERMS: 5 MINUTES PER HOUR,
PER HOUR.
TOTAL TIME OWED: 55,000 YEARS.

Andrew Brown sat down on the ground, and all the other Andrew Browns around the house disappeared.

"Ah, I see you'll decide not to borrow any more time," said the Doctor. "That's the right thing to do when you've already borrowed more than the lives of five hundred people. Wait a minute!" The Doctor put his head to one side as he had an idea. "You owe them more than it's possible to pay back . . . That's very interesting. I wonder if —"

"But I don't understand," Andrew said. "Why didn't the watch tell me when I'd . . ." He suddenly looked angry. "I only borrowed a few days! I don't believe you! But I can check it. If I pay back one per cent of one per cent of what I owe, I should pay back, what, five years?"

"Five and a half," said the Doctor.

"OK," said Andrew. He pressed some buttons on the watch and moved a dial. Then he fell to his knees. Some grey appeared in his hair, and he had some new lines on his face. He looked at himself in his car's mirror.

"Oh, no!" said Andrew. "You're right. But . . . Lots of people are using the watches. How can we stop this?"

"That, Andrew, is where you can help," said the Doctor, and he began to tell Andrew what they knew.

"So, you see," finished the Doctor, "the Mr Symington and Mr Blenkinsop aliens must be storing the time that they've taken from people somewhere. I think they're keeping it on Earth, probably in the bank!"

"I think that I know where it is," said Andrew. "I found some documents when I was looking at some reports – I'll get the papers now." They went into the house.

"Ah! Here they are!" Andrew said when he found the papers in his office upstairs. He pulled a piece of paper out and showed Amy and the Doctor. It was a bill from a company called Little Green Storage for £454,909. "One of those bills comes every month," said Andrew. "They're paid from a bank **account** that I've never seen on any other bills."

Amy took the piece of paper out of Andrew's hands and read it. "But that address can't be right," she said.

"Why?" said the Doctor.

"Because that's the address of the **Millennium Dome**," said Amy. "And there is no storage company there."

"Actually, I've had a storage room there for thousands of years," replied the Doctor. "I've never stored anything in there, but I'm sure I'll store something useful in it one day."

They took a taxi to the Millennium Dome and walked round the outside until they found a very small door. Above the door was a small sign with the words "Little Green Storage" written on it in black pen. It did not look very important.

The Doctor knocked on the door, which soon opened. Then a man's voice said, "Yes?"

"Hello," said the Doctor. "I'm the Doctor, and these are my friends Amy and Andrew, and I was wondering if I could . . ."

"Doctor. Come in," said the voice. "The things in your storage room are quite safe, I promise you."

"Doctor," whispered Amy. "You said that you haven't put anything in your storage room?"

"I haven't," he whispered back. "But in the future I will."

Amy did not know what the Doctor meant. She followed him through the door, on to a **platform** in the air. When Amy looked down, she saw hundreds of floors. Each floor was filled with doors to storage rooms.

"Welcome back to Little Green Storage," said the voice. Then a small man came forward and held out his hand to shake hands with the Doctor. The Doctor moved in a strange way as he shook the man's hand, and Amy felt sure something strange had happened.

"You need to put your secret number in here," the man said, pointing to a **keypad**. "And then you put your **handprint** on the door to open your storage room. I'm sure you remember."

"Of course," said the Doctor, and the man disappeared.

"Andrew, have you got that bill?" asked the Doctor.

Andrew Brown pulled the paper from his pocket. There was a long number under the name of the bank.

"OK," said the Doctor, "let's put in the number and go to the Lexington Bank storage room."

"Wait, Doctor," said Amy. "The small man said we need a handprint, and we can't use yours to get into the bank's storage."

"You're quite right, Amy," the Doctor replied. "We need a handprint, and that could be a big problem." Then he took a long, silver thing out of his pocket. "But I stole the **master key** when I was shaking our friend's hand. Come on!"

He turned back to the keypad and put in the number.

The Mr Symingtons and Mr Blenkinsops had not been able to open the TARDIS door, so now they were going to try something different. Nadia did not hear them talk much, because they seemed to know each other's thoughts.

"We should . . ." said one.

"Yes, possibly," said another.

"Bring it, then," said a third, "and we'll . . ."

". . . break the doors," finished a fourth.

A Mr Symington brought something into the basement and put it carefully on the TARDIS door. It looked like a small, glass half-bubble. In the centre of the bubble, a dial was moving, and numbers were counting down.

"Stand back!" said a Mr Blenkinsop, and all the Mr Symingtons and Mr Blenkinsops covered their ears with their hands. Suddenly, Nadia realized that the half-bubble was a bomb.

CHAPTER EIGHT
Under the Millennium Dome

After the Doctor pressed the last number on the keypad, the platform moved down quickly towards the centre of the underground Dome. They flew past 200 floors of storage rooms and then suddenly stopped in front of a door marked with the same number as Andrew's bill. The Doctor put the master key close to the handprint, and the key changed shape to fill it.

The door unlocked, and they went into a room which was full of **shelves**. Each shelf held a green glass box about the size of a house **brick**. There were thousands of them, and each one had a name on it. There was a strange light moving inside each one. Amy thought she had seen a light like that before, but she could not remember where.

"Well," said the Doctor, "I think we've found the time storage."

In the centre of the room was something that looked like a dentist's chair. It had a belt in the middle.

"How horrible!" he said. "It's a Time-**Harvesting** chair. It would be very hard to get out of that. This is how the aliens take time from people without watches."

Amy touched some of the bricks while Andrew was reading the names on them.

"Be careful with those," the Doctor said to her. "Each one of them is a person's time."

51

"So are these bricks where the aliens are keeping the stolen time?" asked Amy. "If we broke all of them, would everyone get their time back?"

"I'm not sure," said the Doctor.

The Doctor closed his eyes and reached his arms out to the side. He went very quiet and still, and then he opened his eyes again. "No," he said. "Time is very dangerous to keep in storage. If this room was filled with all the time that they've taken from everyone, I'd be able to feel it. These are more like . . . **bank statements**. But there's something strange about the bricks."

The Doctor waved his arms at the walls of green glass.

"Why do the bank statements need to look so beautiful? Maybe they are selling the time as watch-**contracts**. But no one has sold time since the Time War; it's not allowed."

"If we break them all," Amy said, "then no one will owe anything any more."

"Or, if we break them all," replied the Doctor, "everyone will have to pay back what they owe immediately. Or nothing will happen, or it will be the end of the universe. We don't know."

Andrew Brown had been quiet for a long time. He was staring at one brick. On the brick was his name: *Andrew Brown, Lexington Bank.*

"I did it to myself," he said. He reached out and picked up the brick.

The Doctor inspected it. "Do you see that?" he said. There was a very thin line all the way around the glass

brick, near the top. Amy saw that the other bricks had a line around them, too. It looked like a **lid**. The Doctor tried to lift the lid off very carefully, but it did not move.

"So what should we do now, Doctor?" asked Amy.

"I'd like to see what future-me has put in my storage room," said the Doctor.

Andrew put his brick in his pocket, and they left the Lexington storage room. As they went, Amy's camera made a new sound, and a message appeared: **LOW BATTERY. RECHARGE FOR MORE LUCKY MOMENTS.**

"This shouldn't happen!" said Amy "It's a fifty-first-century camera with a cosmic radiation battery that recharges from the energy of the universe! The battery should never get low!" She put it back in her pocket.

Back on the platform, the Doctor put in the number of his storage room into the keypad and the platform flew up to his own room. This time, the Doctor put his own handprint on the door, and they went into the empty room. The only thing inside the room was a closed bag with a page inside it from a magazine, and two batteries.

"This is interesting!" said the Doctor, but he did not explain why.

———

When they got outside the Dome, Amy was very happy to breathe fresh air again. A lot of time had passed while they were in the Dome, and now the sun was coming up. Andrew was looking at the glass brick he had taken.

"Did we learn anything useful, Doctor?" he asked.

"No, not really," the Doctor replied. "We know where the aliens are keeping the bank statements, but we don't know where they are storing the time. We don't even know who let them into the bank at the start."

Andrew turned the brick in his hands. On its bottom, in very small, dark green letters, it said: **IF FOUND, PLEASE RETURN TO THE OFFICE OF VANESSA LAING-RANDALL, LEXINGTON BANK.**

Nadia looked at the faces of the Mr Symingtons and Mr Blenkinsops as they watched the glass time-bomb. She had to get the bomb off the Doctor's TARDIS, and, after that, she knew what she had to do next. Nadia had never used her watch much before it broke. But now it could help her.

She turned the dial on her watch back an hour. Nothing changed, but the clock on the wall said it was an hour earlier. She looked around for something heavy and picked up a big telephone book. Then she waited next to the TARDIS, but, this time, she was there before Mr Symington came to put the bomb on the TARDIS door.

When Mr Symington arrived, she hit him hard on the back of his hand with the heavy book, and the bomb fell to the floor. The Mr Symingtons and Mr Blenkinsops pushed against each other as they tried to catch it, but Nadia was quicker. As she picked the bomb up, she felt it pull her watch, which was making sparks and noise.

The thing inside the bomb was moving fast, and then there was a bright white light. The bomb pulled Nadia's

watch harder, more sparks flew out of it and her hands suddenly grew really, really old.

The Mr Symingtons and Mr Blenkinsops were confused when the TARDIS doors did not open, and they moved away. Feeling much older than she'd ever been before, Nadia walked slowly out of the bank and fell into a strange sleep in the street.

CHAPTER NINE
Earth is losing its future!

"So if all the bricks belong to Vanessa," said Amy, "we have to go back to the bank."

"You and I can't go there," said the Doctor. "The Mr Symingtons and Mr Blenkinsops will still be looking for us. But Andrew can discover what's going on in Vanessa Laing-Randall's office, while we find Nadia Montgomery. I want to look at her watch again."

When Amy and the Doctor found Nadia on a street near the bank, she was talking to herself, and she did not know who they were. They gave her hot chocolate and cheese sandwiches and tried to explain who they were, but Nadia was too old and confused to understand.

The Doctor looked at Nadia's watch. It made sparks sometimes, and sometimes it moved so quickly that it seemed to almost disappear for a moment. He took out the sonic screwdriver and did something to the watch.

"Are you trying to fix it, Doctor?" asked Amy.

"No, I don't want to fix it," he said. "I want it to do something for us. All those Mr Symingtons and Mr Blenkinsops are the same alien, right? Some came later and some came earlier, but they all share memories. They all know they can **ignore** Nadia's watch because it's broken. If we can get her watch to work like an umbrella, we can stay under it, and they'll ignore us, too."

Black smoke came out of Nadia's watch, and she quickly became younger and then older again. The lines on her face disappeared and then appeared again, and her hair grew thicker and then thin. Then, suddenly, there was an orange line around all three of them. It was like a big umbrella made of orange light.

"I've done it!" said the Doctor.

———

Andrew walked towards Sameera's office. She was working at her computer, but she was also at the end of the hall carrying some paperwork. "Why did I not notice before that she was in several places at the same time?" he thought. Lots of people in the bank were doing it, too. Andrew had thought that he was the only one who had too much work to do. But, as he looked, he realized that half the people in the bank were wearing the watches.

When Andrew walked into Sameera's office, she said, "You missed the meeting. Don't worry, I did your presentation for you."

"How much time did you have to borrow to do that?" said Andrew.

Sameera looked at him strangely, and he knew that she was wondering how much he knew. "I only borrowed what I can pay back," she answered, finally.

"Oh, really?" said Andrew. "Do you know about the compound interest?"

"Yes, I do," she said. "I've tried to be careful."

Andrew showed Sameera how to get her watch to tell her what she owed. It said: **BORROWED TIME TOTAL: 5 DAYS, 5 HOURS. INTEREST TERMS: 5 MINUTES PER HOUR, PER HOUR. TOTAL TIME OWED: 35 YEARS.**

"Oh, no!" she cried. "How did that happen? I thought that I was being careful!"

"You've been more careful than me," said Andrew. "I owe 55,000 years. If I pay it back, I'll die. Like Brian Edelman." He told her about Brian touching his watch before falling down dead. Then he showed her his brick. Before now, Sameera had always seemed like his enemy, but now he felt sorry for her.

"I always tried to pay it back after a few hours," she said. "I knew that the interest would be a problem if I didn't pay it quickly. But I've been so busy, and . . ."

Andrew nodded. "There were so many meetings where I felt like you were more prepared than me."

"But I wasn't!" Sameera said. "Sometimes I had to leave to go and borrow the time so I could come back prepared!"

"I did the same thing," said Andrew.

Sameera nodded sadly and stared through her office window at the glass atrium sculpture.

"We did this to each other," she said. "And now we've got to fix it before more people die."

———

Amy held Nadia's hand. Nadia was about sixty years old now, and she was getting older. "The only way to stop this is to take that watch off her wrist," said the Doctor.

"I could get older and younger, too, couldn't I, Doctor?" Amy asked in a worried voice. "Now that my watch is broken like Nadia's."

"Maybe," the Doctor said. "But, I think we have something worse to worry about. Show me your camera again."

Amy pulled the Special Lucky Holiday Camera out of her pocket. A message on it said: **PLEASE RECHARGE!**

"It should have **infinite** battery life," he said.

"That's what they told me in the shop when I bought it," said Amy.

The Doctor took out the bag he had taken from the storage room. It had a magazine **article** and some batteries inside. "It's a Time Bag," he said. "The bag stops time affecting the things inside it. Imagine I put you in this bag, closed it and then went into the past and murdered your grandfather. You'd be OK if you stayed in the bag. If I opened the bag, you would disappear like you never **existed**. While the magazine article is in the bag, changes in time can't affect it. When we take it out, it will probably change."

Amy looked at the article inside the bag. It was written in the year 5013 about the **inventor** of the cosmic radiation battery – like the one in Amy's camera. Henrietta Nwokolo, the article said, had **invented** the battery at Aberdeen University. The article also said that people in Japan and Australia had invented cosmic radiation batteries, too, but their batteries often needed recharging. Under the article was an advertisement for Amy's Special Lucky Holiday Camera, with its cosmic radiation battery that never needed recharging.

"Let's see," said the Doctor. "What's going to happen if we take the article out of the bag?"

Amy opened the bag, and she immediately saw the words on the article change. It was still about the inventor of the battery, but now, the inventor was Kyumi Yamamoto at Tokyo University. And it said the technology was important, but it was not perfect because the battery often needed recharging.

The Doctor gave her the batteries from the Time Bag. "These will recharge your camera," he said, "but maybe not for long, so be careful when you use them."

Amy nodded and put the batteries into the Special Lucky Holiday Camera. She stared at the magazine. "But why did the article change, Doctor?"

"It means," he said, "that the future is changing. The people who made your camera's technology will never be born because their parents will never be born. Their time was stolen from them. Earth is losing its future. The more time the aliens take from people, the more they can move around in time. Then they can go really far back into the past and steal time from even more people. They'll take all the time that Earth ever had, until Earth stops existing."

CHAPTER TEN
Amy has a plan

Amy and the Doctor walked slowly with Nadia into the back door of the bank under the safe orange umbrella of the broken watch. Ordinary people could see them, but the aliens could not. While they waited in an empty meeting room for Andrew and Sameera to finish searching the bank, Amy switched on the television. "Today, the Chancellor of the Exchequer will be speaking at Lexington Bank," the woman on the news was saying.

Nadia's watch was making purple and green sparks, and she was getting younger and younger. It had happened many times before, but each time, it felt terribly wrong.

"I don't know how to tell you this, but you're about ten years old," said the Doctor. "We'll have to fix it, but not right now."

"Doctor," Amy said and pointed at the television. "Look at her arm." The woman reading the news was wearing one of the alien watches. They watched her in shock. The watches were everywhere! They saw one on the wrist of the mayor of a town in South America who was talking about his successes in the fight against crime. A team of scientists in Iceland, who had made a discovery about energy, were all wearing them, too.

"They're doing some good things with the watches, Doctor," said Amy.

"Yes," said the Doctor. "You can do a lot of amazing things with extra time. That's the trouble with borrowing. It makes everything look good. No one wants to see what's really going on because it all looks so pretty. But it's no good making everything pretty, if everyone will die when they pay back their borrowed time."

Amy nodded, slowly. "We have to find a way to tell the world about the watches," she said. "And I think I know when we'll have the perfect chance."

———

Andrew and Sameera stood behind some plants on the tenth floor and watched a Mr Symington and a Mr Blenkinsop walk down the hall. "Let's see where they go," said Sameera. "We've got time before we meet Amy and the Doctor."

Mr Symington and Mr Blenkinsop knocked on the door of Vanessa Laing-Randall's office and walked straight in without waiting. Sameera and Andrew waited for a long time, but the aliens did not come out again.

"We need to see inside that office," said Andrew. "The bricks belong to Vanessa, and Mr Symington and Mr Blenkinsop are doing something in there."

They went into Vanessa's office, but there was no one in there.

"Where did Vanessa, Mr Symington and Mr Blenkinsop go?" asked Sameera.

"Maybe," Andrew said, "we didn't see them because they travelled back in time before we arrived."

They searched Vanessa's desk and checked her computer quickly. There was not any evidence of what they planned to do with all the stolen time, but then Andrew noticed a locked door at the back of the office.

He was looking for its key when a woman's voice made them jump. "What do you think you're doing?" the voice said. It was Vanessa, and she did not look pleased to see them.

"We know what you're doing here!" Sameera said to Vanessa. "We know everything about the watches, about you lending time, and about Time Harvesting!"

"And we know about these!" said Andrew, and he held his brick up for her to see.

Vanessa's eyes opened in shock, but then she smiled quickly.

"I don't know what you're talking about," she said. "But I think we should have a meeting about it. How about tomorrow in this office? At ten o'clock?"

Suddenly, the locked door at the back of the office opened, and Mr Symington and Mr Blenkinsop came in.

"OK," said Andrew, moving backwards. "Ten o'clock!" He pulled Sameera out of the office with him. "Run!" he said, and they ran.

Vanessa stood and watched them leave. "Follow them," she said to Mr Symington and Mr Blenkinsop. "I want to know how they found that brick. Someone must be helping them, and I want to know who it is."

Andrew and Sameera met the Doctor, Amy and a little girl in the meeting room. They could see a thin orange line around the Doctor and Amy from Nadia's watch.

"You brought a child with you . . . to a bank full of aliens?" Sameera asked.

"I'm not a child," Nadia said. "I'm the Head of Communications. My watch is broken, and it made me younger."

"Oh, OK," said Sameera. "You must be Nadia Montgomery, then?"

"Anyway," said Andrew, after he had explained what had happened in Vanessa's office. "We thought Mr Symington and Mr Blenkinsop would follow us, but they didn't. Do you think they're planning something, Doctor?"

"Probably," replied the Doctor.

"What's our plan, Doctor?" asked Sameera. "How are we going to stop them and save everyone who's wearing those watches?"

"It's not just the people with the watches," Amy said. "We have to save Earth's future."

The Doctor looked towards the centre of the atrium, with its huge twisted-glass sculpture. He stared up at it.

"We have to let the world know what's going on, before everyone starts wearing those watches," said Amy. "The Chancellor's meeting is going to be on television. Sameera and Andrew can take us in to the meeting, can't you? Then we can tell the world what's really happening at Lexington Bank."

———————

Outside the meeting room, two men in black suits were listening to Amy.

"How very interesting, don't you think, Mr Symington?" said Mr Blenkinsop.

"Very interesting," said Mr Symington. "We can only see two people in the room, but we can hear five people talking."

"And they have a plan," said Mr Blenkinsop. "I think we need to stop them from achieving that plan."

"We will, Mr Blenkinsop," replied Mr Symington. "We will."

CHAPTER ELEVEN

The Doctor saves everyone except himself

On the stage in the library of Lexington Bank, the Chancellor of the Exchequer was starting his speech. "I'm very happy," the Chancellor said, "to be here today at Lexington Bank . . ."

In front of the stage, there were lots of chairs filled with people from the bank. Television cameras were there, too, to **broadcast** the speech **live** all over the world. Andrew and Sameera were sitting on chairs at the front of the room, near the stage. Amy, the Doctor and Nadia stood at the back of the room next to the television cameras, safe under the orange light of Nadia's watch. It was strange, but they could not see Vanessa or any Mr Symingtons or Mr Blenkinsops anywhere.

Amy suddenly ran towards the stage. The Chancellor stopped speaking when Amy jumped in front of him. The Doctor and Nadia followed close behind Amy and waited by the side of the stage.

"Aliens are here, and they're controlling everything," shouted Amy. "They're giving everybody watches like these." She held up her arm to show the watch to the cameras.

Two tall men in black suits quietly helped the Chancellor off the stage and out of the library. Amy realized that she must sound crazy, so she pulled ten-year-old Nadia on to the stage. "Nadia, tell them what happened to you!" said Amy. Nadia looked straight into the cameras.

She held up her red arm, with the sparks still flying out of the watch. "Six months ago," she said, "I was forty years old. But I was stupid. I borrowed time using this watch. Look at me now!" She shook her wrist angrily.

But shaking the broken watch was not a good idea. It made some more sparks and a loud sound, and then its face went black. Nadia stared at it in shock. The orange line around the Doctor, Amy and Nadia disappeared. Suddenly, the room was full of Mr Symingtons and Mr Blenkinsops who had travelled back in time to appear there. The Mr Symingtons and Mr Blenkinsops could all see Amy, Nadia and the Doctor now.

At that moment, Sameera jumped on to the stage and pressed some buttons on her watch to pay back her time. In one terrible moment, the watch took thirty-five years of her life. She could immediately feel the thousand different pains of being old, but she kept looking at the camera. "This is what the aliens have done to me," she said.

At the same time, the Mr Symingtons and Mr Blenkinsops all began to run towards Amy with sharks' faces. She took her camera and tried to catch some of them inside Time Bubbles, but more and more of them were coming. Andrew and Sameera started fighting the shark-men, too. They threw chairs and television cameras at them. Most of the other people in the bank were not fighting; they

were running out of the library. Sameera was not very strong now, but she still threw a chair at a Mr Symington. She hit him in the mouth, and immediately, all the other Mr Symingtons in the room had blood on their mouths. Andrew threw a chair, but one of the Mr Blenkinsops caught it and threw it back. The sharks seemed to know what would happen before it happened.

"They're remembering how we are fighting!" shouted the Doctor. "Look at those ones at the side of the room!" He pointed to a Mr Symington and a Mr Blenkinsop standing at the side of the library without any blood on their faces.

"That's the first Mr Symington and Mr Blenkinsop! When they see something, all the others remember it! Catch those two with your camera, Amy!"

Amy turned the camera towards them. But it had a message on it: **ONLY ONE LUCKY HOLIDAY MOMENT LEFT. CHOOSE CAREFULLY!** "What if we need this last bubble later?" she asked herself.

The shark-men knew that she would stop and think because they had already seen her do it. Three Mr Blenkinsops quickly jumped forward and pushed Amy to the ground. Amy screamed and kicked as a Mr Blenkinsop opened its mouth wide to bite her.

"No!" shouted the Doctor.

"She agreed to the terms and conditions," said Mr Symington. He held Amy's wrist and pressed buttons on her watch. The message said: **BORROWED TIME TOTAL: 21 YEARS, 1 MONTH, 16 DAYS.** It had gone up since the last time she had looked at it.

"Take me instead," said the Doctor. "Your boss won't be interested in normal people like Amy any more when you tell her that I know the Time Market."

Suddenly, all the fighting stopped, and all the Mr Symingtons and Mr Blenkinsops were still and silent. And then the lift doors opened, and Vanessa Laing-Randall walked out.

"You can let Amy go now," said the Doctor, gently. "You and I can talk about your business instead."

"Oh, Doctor," said Vanessa. "You don't understand anything."

"You can't win, Vanessa!" shouted Sameera. "Everyone in the world has seen me get older! Everyone knows what you're doing, and no one will borrow any more time from you."

Vanessa shook her head. "Nobody outside this bank saw anything," she said. "We heard about your plans, and we stopped the live broadcast. You can't stop me like that. We will always be able to time travel and stay one step ahead of you."

Sameera looked like she wanted to cry.

"So, Doctor." Vanessa smiled. "What were you saying to my friends here about the Time Market?"

"They're not really your friends," said the Doctor. "You're all the same alien. Are you the earliest one?"

Vanessa smiled. The Mr Symingtons and Mr Blenkinsops smiled, too. "Oh, you're so, so clever," she said. "I wonder how you knew. I must remember to go back in time and stop you from discovering our secret. Yes, I'm the first. I'm like a tree, and my sharks are the branches. Aren't they lovely?"

"That's a nice sculpture," said the Doctor instead, staring at the glass shape in the atrium. "I think maybe I'm beginning to understand. Not many people have paid you back the time they owe you yet, have they? You haven't actually got much time at all, not really." At that moment, a Mr Blenkinsop pulled Amy's arm and held it behind her back until she screamed.

"What were you saying about the Time Market?" Vanessa repeated.

The Doctor stared at Vanessa. "If I tell you what I know," he said, "will you let me pay the time Amy owes you?"

Vanessa pressed a button on Amy's watch. "She owes me twenty-one years. That's a lot! But you can pay it for her if you want to."

The Mr Blenkinsop made Amy walk to the Doctor and hold up her watch arm. "Press this button here to pay it for her," Vanessa said. "Be careful, Doctor – twenty-one years at the same time hurts, you know."

The Doctor looked at Vanessa and pressed the button. Amy's watch fell to the floor, and the glass face broke into a hundred pieces. The Doctor did not look or feel any older.

"I don't understand. You didn't get older . . ." For the first time, Vanessa did not know what to say.

The Doctor said nothing. All the Mr Symingtons and Mr Blenkinsops were staring at him with excitement.

"You can't be . . ." Vanessa whispered. "I thought all the Time Lords were gone!"

The Mr Symingtons and Mr Blenkinsops were suddenly standing in front of all the library's exits.

"Doctor, what's going on?" asked Amy.

The Doctor smiled at Amy. "I think our friend the Time Harvester here has just thought of a way to achieve a lot of success on the Time Market." Then he said to Vanessa, "Will you let Andrew go if I wear one of your watches?"

"You would wear a watch? I don't understand," said Vanessa.

"Andrew owes you more than 55,000 years. So why don't you put a watch on me and take his time from me instead? And then we'll talk about the future of the Earth."

"I . . ." Vanessa opened and closed her mouth, and then she stopped talking.

A Mr Symington took a watch from his pocket and put it around the Doctor's wrist. Andrew's watch fell to the floor.

"You're both free now," said the Doctor. "You don't owe any time, and you can't borrow any more time, Amy and Andrew. Sameera, I'm sure you don't want to use your watch again! And . . ." The Doctor nodded his head at the huge glass sculpture and spoke so quietly that only Amy could hear him. "And I think that sculpture is what Sameera calls a **liquidity fund**. It's time to break it."

A Mr Symington and a Mr Blenkinsop put a cold hand on each of the Doctor's shoulders.

"You must come with us now, Doctor," said Vanessa.

"I know some people at the Time Market who'll be very excited to see you."

It was terrible to watch Vanessa and her army of Mr Symingtons and Mr Blenkinsops lead the Doctor across the atrium. At the door, a Mr Blenkinsop took several things from the Doctor's pockets and put them on the floor. Then, Vanessa turned a dial on the Doctor's watch, and they all disappeared.

The whole bank was empty now because everyone had run away from the fighting. There were only a few Mr Symingtons and Mr Blenkinsops, and they did not stop Amy, Sameera and Andrew from sitting in the atrium next to the glass sculpture.

"So the Doctor wants us to break some **advanced** alien technology?" said Andrew. Amy noticed that Andrew's hand was on sixty-five-year-old Sameera's shoulder.

"The Doctor said that the sculpture is a 'liquidity fund'," Amy said, "but I don't know what that is."

Andrew and Sameera looked at each other. "I'll explain," said Sameera. "Most people are still wearing the watches and walking around like nothing strange is happening. They owe time, but they haven't paid it back yet. Vanessa will have that time later because people owe it to her, but she doesn't have it yet, so she can't use it now."

"OK," said Amy. "So how can the Mr Symingtons and Mr Blenkinsops move in time when not enough people have paid the time they owe Vanessa?"

"She must have some in storage somewhere that she

can use when she needs to travel in time," said Andrew. "We call that kind of storage a liquidity fund."

"So if we broke the liquidity fund . . ." said Amy, "people would still owe Vanessa their time if they have borrowed from her."

"But it would be harder for Vanessa and her sharks to move backwards and forwards in time," continued Sameera.

"If the Doctor thinks that sculpture is the liquidity fund where Vanessa is keeping her time," Amy said, "then let's break it."

CHAPTER TWELVE
The Time Market

Vanessa took the Doctor to the storage room under the Millennium Dome and made him sit in the Time-Harvesting chair. Then she broadcast from a camera in the storage room to the Time Market **trading** hall, far away somewhere in the universe. Inside, hundreds of different kinds of alien **traders** were watching computers above their heads.

"I know many of you have bought and sold, and made money from, my watch-contracts," Vanessa said to the traders, and she pointed to the glass bricks on the shelves. "But now, I have something even better for you. This is the last of the Time Lords."

A shocked whisper went around the Time Market. "A Time Lord!"

"How much will you pay for him?" Vanessa asked them.

The aliens in the Time Market immediately started shouting numbers. Trading had begun.

Then someone asked, "Wait, how do we know he's really a Time Lord?"

In the storage room, Vanessa turned to the Doctor. "Show them that you're a Time Lord," she ordered.

"No," he said and smiled.

Amy was standing on the **balcony** of the tenth floor of the bank, and she was looking down on to the glass sculpture.

Andrew, Sameera and Nadia were pushing a heavy metal cupboard towards the balcony.

"Push harder," said Amy. "We've got to do this before anyone sees us."

Then a voice said, "Oh dear."

Amy turned to see a Mr Blenkinsop just behind her. Suddenly, there were Mr Symingtons and Mr Blenkinsops everywhere. Some of them still looked like men, and some of them had already become sharks. Amy had an idea. She took the Special Lucky Holiday Camera, but she did not point it towards the Mr Symingtons and Mr Blenkinsops. She pointed it at herself, Andrew, Sameera, Nadia and the cupboard. Then she pressed the button down and ran forward, towards the balcony.

A Time Bubble came out of the camera and grew longer and longer as she ran. When she reached the balcony, she threw the camera over the side. The camera **hung** in the air from its Time Bubble. Nadia, Andrew and Sameera and the cupboard were all safe inside the bubble.

The bubble hung above the glass sculpture.

"Wow!" said Andrew. "That is clever."

"Come on," Amy said. "We need to move the cupboard before the bubble disappears."

"You've borrowed a lot of time from the market, haven't you?" the Doctor asked Vanessa.

Vanessa did not seem worried. "Now I've got you, I'll get all my time back and more," she told him.

"You've borrowed more time than those watch-contracts are actually worth," the Doctor guessed.

"Things are worth what people will pay for them," Vanessa said. "The traders want to pay a lot for those contracts, and for you."

The Doctor smiled and said nothing.

———————

Amy, Andrew and Nadia moved the cupboard as quickly as they could. They lifted it and pushed it over the balcony so that it hung in the air above the glass sculpture. Then the bubble started to disappear, and everything happened at the same time.

The camera fell down the ten floors of Lexington Bank and broke on the ground. A Mr Symington and a Mr Blenkinsop caught Amy and held her down on the floor. Amy kicked and screamed as Mr Blenkinsop began to bite into her arm. Andrew and Sameera and Nadia were also about to become shark food. Very slowly, the cupboard started to fall. Some of the Mr Symingtons and Mr Blenkinsops moved to stop it, but it was too late. The cupboard hit the glass sculpture, and huge pieces of broken glass flew everywhere. The light in the middle of the sculpture disappeared and, at the same time, all the Mr Symingtons and all the Mr Blenkinsops suddenly disappeared, too.

In the Time Market, Vanessa felt the sharks leave. She was confused for a moment, and then she tried to go back in time to stop the cupboard hitting her liquidity fund, but she could not move. Her liquidity fund had gone, and now she had no more time. She was suddenly very frightened.

"Traders of the Time Market," said the Doctor to the aliens. "I'm not really a Time Lord. I don't even know what a Time Lord is."

"He's lying!" Vanessa shouted.

"I'm not lying," said the Doctor. "Vanessa's lying – and I can show you how. Look at the other things she's sold you on this market, like the watch-contracts. The glass bricks look good, don't they?" He pointed at the bricks on the shelves of the storage room. "But this watch shows how much Andrew Brown owes. He owes more than 55,000 years. He borrowed more time than he can pay back, like a lot of people who used the watches."

The Doctor held his watch up so the alien traders could all see its face. He watched them think about it. Fifty-five thousand years was a lot of time, but it was only about ten per cent of a human life – or that's what Vanessa had told them. People on Earth could pay it back easily, but if they did not pay, the contract said you could take their life instead.

"Check your computers," ordered the Doctor. "See how long a human life is."

"No!" shouted Vanessa. "Don't listen to him."

The aliens checked their computers for the information and tried to understand what they were reading. And, as soon as they understood the truth, they all started shouting, "Sell! Sell! Sell!"

As the price of the watch-contracts fell lower and lower, traders tried to sell them to other traders. Then there came a moment when Vanessa was worth so little that she could not trade any more. She had no time left in her liquidity, and no one wanted to give her any time for her watch-contracts.

The things she had done with the time she had borrowed started to disappear. Some of the glass bricks disappeared because the Mr Symingtons and Mr Blenkinsops who had put those watches on people's wrists had never existed.

"Stop trading!" Vanessa cried out. "I admit that I lied about how long humans live, but this is a real Time Lord, with a TARDIS! Just stop, and listen to me! I can sell you more time than you can imagine!"

But it was too late. If Vanessa had lied to them about the humans, then what other lies had she told them? They tried to sell everything they had ever bought from her, but no one was buying.

Vanessa suddenly disappeared like she had never existed. Had she kept a small bit of time for herself somewhere? The Doctor stood up from the Time-Harvesting chair and looked at the camera.

"I'm the Doctor," he said. The Time Market went quiet. "We all know trading time is not allowed," he continued. "I don't care about any of you, but I do care very much about the people on Earth. I'll buy your Earth time-contracts for, let's say, one second for every ten years."

The aliens all sold him their contracts as fast as possible. Soon, all the green, glass bricks that were left in the storage room belonged to the Doctor.

No one at Lexington Bank knew how the sculpture broke, but everyone who was still wearing a watch got a message that said: **YOU NO LONGER OWE ANY TIME.**

On the top floor of the building, Amy, Andrew, Sameera and Nadia were waiting for the Doctor to return. "What am I going to do?" said Nadia. "I can't get a job for another ten years!"

Then the Doctor suddenly arrived. But this time, there were no Mr Blenkinsops, Mr Symingtons or Vanessa with him. "Sorry I'm late," he said.

They all listened to his story about what had happened at the Time Market, and then they told him how they had broken the glass sculpture. There was only one problem left. The Doctor had a bag with him, and now he put it on the table. The old lady that was Sameera and the little girl Nadia looked at the Doctor with hope in their faces.

"I can't give you any extra time, Sameera," he said, sadly. "It's gone because you've already paid it back."

"Oh," said Sameera.

The Doctor continued. "Those contracts really were awful. Vanessa even added interest as a **penalty** for paying it all back early. Here's your brick," he said, and he took one of the glass bricks out of his bag. "It says you still owe ten years."

The Doctor put another brick next to it. "This one's yours, Nadia," he said. "It seems that your broken watch has done some very strange things to the contract. The contract says you have thirty years of **credit** left. But if you take that credit now, you will go back to before you were born."

"So you can't do anything to help me?" Nadia asked. "I'll have to explain to my parents why I'm ten years old?"

"There is one thing I could do," the Doctor said. He looked at the two bricks, side by side. "Only you can open your own bricks," he said.

Nadia and Sameera both carefully lifted their bricks' glass lids. The Doctor reached inside and pulled out two glass light-balls. He stared at the light-balls, one in his right hand, the other in his left.

"This one says you owe ten years," he said and nodded at Sameera's ball on the right, "and this one says you have thirty years' credit. So, how about if we change them?"

He put each ball into the other brick and put the lids back on. And, suddenly, Sameera was thirty-five, and Nadia was twenty.

After Amy and the Doctor had left in the TARDIS, Andrew and Sameera sat and talked.

"Do you still want that promotion?" Andrew asked.

"I know it sounds stupid," Sameera said. "But I don't want to work in a bank any more. I'd like to be a manager in a restaurant in a town with a beach. What about you?"

"I always wanted to be a music teacher," Andrew said.

"So," she said, "let's do it." And then they kissed and walked out of Lexington Bank forever.

During-reading questions

Write the answers to these questions in your notebook.

CHAPTER ONE

1 What do Mr Symington and Mr Blenkinsop say they can do to fix Andrew's problems?
2 What is special about . . .
   a Amy's camera?
   b the camera's battery?

CHAPTER TWO

1 What does Brian Edelman do before he dies?
2 What reason does Vanessa give for Brian's death?

CHAPTER FOUR

1 In this chapter, what does Amy think is the "price" of one hour of time if she borrows it with the watch?
2 What does Amy do with all the time she borrows?

CHAPTER FIVE

1 How much time . . .
   a does Amy think she has to pay in interest?
   b does she really owe?
2 How does Amy's memory change when they run past the restaurant?

CHAPTER SIX

1 What does Nadia's watch do because it is broken? What happens to Nadia when it does this?
2 Why does the Doctor want to speak to Andrew Brown?
3 What happens when Amy hits one of the sharks with the stone?

CHAPTER EIGHT

1 Describe the Time-Harvesting chair. What is it used for?
2 How does Nadia stop the bomb breaking the TARDIS, and what happens to her?

CHAPTER NINE

1 Why do the aliens ignore Nadia most of the time?
2 How was Sameera more careful with borrowing time than Andrew?

CHAPTER TEN

1 What does the "orange umbrella" that comes out of Nadia's watch do?
2 When Amy says that some people are doing good things with the time they borrow, the Doctor says: "That's the trouble with borrowing. It makes everything look good." What does he mean?
3 Why does Vanessa let Andrew and Sameera go?

CHAPTER ELEVEN

1 When Amy and Nadia tell their stories, what are the people in the library thinking, do you think?
2 Are the shark-men easy or difficult to fight? Explain your answer.

CHAPTER TWELVE

1 Why won't the Doctor show the traders that he is a real Time Lord?
2 What does Amy use her last Time Bubble for?
3 What does the Doctor do to make Sameera and Nadia the correct ages again?

After-reading questions

1 Who is your favourite person in the story? Why?

2 Would the watches be a good idea if the interest was not compound interest? Give reasons for your answer.

3 What have you learned about the world of international banking from reading this book?

4 What does the story say about working long hours, do you think? Is it a good thing or a bad thing to work long hours?

Exercises

1 Write the correct word in your notebook.

1 romntpooi .... *promotion* .... Getting a better job in the
same company.

2 ontraepesnti A kind of speech that people make at work.

3 bebulb A round thing that you can see through.

4 reyabtt A thing that gives electricity to machines.

5 towrh How special or good something is.

6 useeivnr The name for all the planets and stars together.

7 RASTID What the Doctor uses to travel in time.

2 **Write the correct verb form, past simple or past perfect, in your notebook.**

1 Nadia *looked* / **had looked** very tired, like she **did not sleep** / **had not slept** for days.

2 Amy thought that Brian Edelman **touched** / **had touched** something on his wrist before he **died** / **had died**.

3 A secretary **covered** / **had covered** Brian Edelman's face with a coat by the time the Doctor and Amy **got** / **had got** to his office.

4 Andrew's presentation **was** / **had been** good because he **spent** / **had spent** a lot of time preparing it.

5 Amy **found** / **had found** Sameera's lunch receipts before Sameera **discovered** / **had discovered** her.

6 Sameera **thought** / **had thought** that Amy **borrowed** / **had borrowed** time with a watch too.

CHAPTER SIX

3 **Who is thinking this? Write the correct name in your notebook.**

Amy	Nadia	the Doctor
	Mr Symington and Mr Blenkinsop	

1 "Where did she just come from?" .Mr Symington and Mr Blenkinsop.

2 "I hate it in here. It makes me feel so confused."

3 "We must try and open the doors of this blue box."

4 "I don't understand what the Doctor's talking about!"

5 "Good! Now we know something very useful about the aliens."

6 "I think Andrew Brown could help us!"

4 **Are these sentences *true* or *false*? Write the answers in your notebook.**

1 Andrew has paid back all of the time he has borrowed.....*false*.....

2 It is impossible for Andrew to pay back all the time he has borrowed.

3 The Doctor steals a master key for all the storage rooms.

4 Amy's camera works better while they are under the Dome.

5 Nadia saves the TARDIS from the aliens.

5 **Complete these sentences in your notebook, using the words or phrases from the box.**

shelves	lid	article
bricks	contract	bank statement

Inside the storage room, the Doctor, Amy and Andrew find
¹.........*shelves*......... full of green, glass ²............ Each one is a
kind of ³..........., and everyone who has a signed a watch-⁴...........
with the aliens has one. There is a light inside but the Doctor
cannot open the ⁵........... to look more closely. The Doctor's own
storage room contains a Time Bag with an ⁶........... in it.

CHAPTER TWELVE

6 **Order the story by writing 1–8 in your notebook.**

a .... The Doctor said he was not a Time Lord.

b .... Vanessa disappeared.

c .... Andrew and Sameera decided they did not want
a promotion.

d .... The Doctor bought all the watch-contracts at a very cheap price.

e .... The watch-contracts became worth almost nothing.

f ......*1*...... Vanessa tried to sell the Doctor to the traders in the Time Market.

g .... Sameera and Nadia changed ages for the last time.

h .... Amy, Andrew, Nadia and Sameera broke Vanessa's liquidity fund.

Project work

1 In 2008, there was an international "banking crisis". Find out about this online, and then think about the story you have just read. How does *Doctor Who: Borrowed Time* show the things that happened in 2008? Write a short presentation.

2 Imagine you have a Special Lucky Holiday Camera: Catch the Moment™. Where would you go, and what moments would you "catch" with it? Write a description of one of the scenes you catch with the camera.

3 Write a newspaper report about what happens in Chapter Eleven.

4 Write a letter from Andrew, Sameera or Nadia to Amy some time after the end of the story. How did their lives change after Amy and the Doctor left?

5 Write a review of this book. Did you like it? Why/Why not?

An answer key for all questions and exercises can be found at **www.penguinreaders.co.uk**

Glossary

account (n.)
When you have a bank *account*, the bank keeps your money and you can take some out when you need it.

advanced (adj.)
very modern or new

alien technology (n.)
machines made by aliens

article (n.)
a story in a newspaper or magazine

assistant (n.)
someone whose job is to help another person with their work

atrium (n.)
a large open space with a glass roof and walls

balcony (n.)
a place above the ground where you can stand outside a building

bank statement (n.)
information on a computer or on paper that tells you how much money is in your bank *account*

bare (adj.)
Something that is *bare* has nothing covering it.

basement (n.)
part of a building that is under the ground

be worth (phr.)
to be as good as

boss (n.)
a person who controls the activities of a company or part of a company and tells other people at work what they must do

brick (n.)
a hard piece of stone with straight sides, used for building

broadcast (v.)
to send out sounds and pictures on TV or radio

bubble (n.)
in this story, a large round ball made of glass or plastic that you can see through

career ladder (phr.)
If someone climbs the *career ladder*, they try to achieve more and more success in their job. (Your *career* is all the jobs that you do through your life. A *ladder* is a thing that you put against a wall and climb up to reach high places.)

Chancellor of the Exchequer (pr. n.)
an important person whose job is to decide how to spend the country's money

client (n.)
someone who pays you to do a job for them

compound interest (n.)
When a bank lends you money, you must pay the money back, but you must also pay the bank some extra money, called *interest*. If the bank also makes you pay extra money on this *interest*, it is called *compound interest*.

confused (adj.)
When you are *confused*, you do not understand what is happening.

contract (n.)
an important document showing that two people have agreed on something

cosmic radiation battery (n.)
in this story, an object that people put in a camera or phone, for example. It uses *energy* from the *universe* to make the camera or phone work.

credit (n.)
If your bank *account* has *credit*, or if it is in *credit*, you are allowed to have that money because it is yours. You have not borrowed it from the bank.

deactivate (v.)
to stop something from working

demonstration (n.)
You give a *demonstration* when you show people how something works.

dial (n.)
a round object on a machine with a needle (= long, thin part) that moves around to show an amount of something

energy (n.)
something like gas that makes heat or light, or that makes things work

evidence (n.)
You use *evidence* to show people that something is true.

exist (v.)
to be alive in this world

gossip (n.)
conversations about other people's private lives

handprint (n.)
a mark in the shape of
someone's hand

hang (v.)
to be attached to something only
at the top, so that the bottom part
can move freely

harvester (n.); **harvest** (v.)
When you *harvest* something,
you collect it. Farmers *harvest* all
the things they have grown. A
harvester is a machine that collects
something.

Head of Communications
(pr. n.)
an important person in a
company who makes sure that
the company talks to customers
and the media well

icing (n.)
a thick cover of sugar on a cake

ignore (v.)
If you *ignore* something, you do
not look at it or care about it.

impress (v.)
If you *impress* someone, you do
something very well so that
they like you or want to work
with you.

infinite (adj.)
Something that is *infinite*
continues for ever.

in person (phr.)
If you do something *in person*,
you go to a place to do it; you do
not do it by writing a message or
making a call.

inspect (v.)
to look at something carefully to
see if it is correct or good enough

interest rate (n.)
Interest is the amount of extra
money you pay to a bank when
you have borrowed money from
it. The *interest rate* is this amount
described as, for example, 3%.

inventor (n.); **invent** (v.)
If you *invent* something, you think
of a new thing that no one has
ever made before, and make it. A
person who does this is an *inventor*.

keypad (n.)
a set of buttons showing
numbers next to a door or on a
small machine. You must *press*
the correct numbers to make
the door open or to make the
machine work.

lid (n.)
a hard cover for something like a
box or a case

liquidity fund (n.)
an amount of money saved in a
bank that you can take out again
quickly and easily. In this story, it
is time, not money, that is saved.

live (adj.)
When a show is *broadcast live*, people can watch it or listen to it while it is happening.

manager (n.)
someone whose job is to control the activities of part of a company and the people who work there

master key (n.)
a key that opens all the doors in a building

memory (n.)
something that you remember happening in the past

Millennium Dome (pr. n.)
a large, round building in London

mystery (n.)
something that is difficult to explain or get information about

name badge (n.)
a small piece of plastic with your name on it that you attach to your clothes on your chest

owe (v.)
If you *owe* someone something (usually money), it means you have borrowed it from them and must pay it back.

penalty (n.)
If someone gives you a *penalty*, they punish you for doing something wrong.

platform (n.)
a flat area that you can stand on above the ground

poor (adj.)
You say that someone is a *poor* child, man or woman, for example, when you feel sad for them.

prepared (adj.)
ready and able to do something well

presentation (n.)
When you give a *presentation*, you describe or explain something to a group of people in a formal way

press (v.)
to push something down

promotion (n.)
when someone moves to a higher position in a company

recharge (v.)
to put more *energy* into a battery (= an object that you put into a small machine such as a camera to make it work)

sculpture (n.)
a large piece of art made of stone or metal, for example

shark (n.)
a large fish that lives in the sea. *Sharks* may bite people.

shelf (n.)
a flat piece of wood that is attached to a wall. People often put books on a *shelf*.

spark (n.)
a very small bright light that flies out of something that is burning or making *energy*

store (v.); **storage** (n.)
If you *store* something, you keep it in a place so that you can use it later. *Storage* is where you *store* things.

TARDIS (pr. n.)
In the *Doctor Who* stories, people travel through time in the TARDIS. It looks like an old telephone box on the outside, but it is very big inside.

tax (n.)
the money that people must give to the government (= the people who control their country) to pay for things like hospitals, schools and roads

terms and conditions (phr.)
a document you must read when you buy or use something. It tells you what you must do, and what you can and cannot do.

time traveller (n.)
someone who travels forward or back in time

trading (n.); **trader** (n.)
Trading is the activity of buying and selling something. People who do this are *traders*.

twisted (adj.)
Things that are *twisted* around each other have grown or been moved so that they turn around each other.

universe (n.)
this world and everything outside it, like the sun and the moon

voicemail (n.)
a voice message from someone on your phone

wonder (v.)
to ask yourself something

wrist (n.)
the part of your arm where it joins your hand. You could wear a bracelet or a watch on your *wrist*.